Book 1
Malware
By Solis Tech

&

Book 2
Robotics
By Kenneth Fraser

&

Book 3
Cryptography
By Solis Tech

Book 1
Malware
By Solis Tech

Malware Detection & Threats Made Easy!

Malware: Malware Detection & Threats Made Easy!

Table of Contents

Introduction

I want to thank you and congratulate you for purchasing the book, *"Malware: Malware Detection & Threats Made Easy!"*.

This book contains proven steps and strategies on how to avoid, detect and remove malware.

Malware creators are very creative, employing both technical and social means to spread malware. Simply installing antivirus software is no longer enough. This book explains how malware spreads in order to arm the reader with information on how to manage its threat.

Thanks again for purchasing this book, I hope you enjoy it!

Chapter 1 – Malware

Computers are inherently dumb. They can accept and input data, can process it at high-speed, and can return the results almost instantly. However, users need to tell the computer what to do in the form of codes. We call these codes programs, applications, scripts or software, but they are essentially the same. They give instructions to the computer. What the computer does will depend on the instructions given to it. Tell it to do something useful and it will. Give it instructions to perform a malicious task and it will do it without question. Even computers with artificial intelligence are simply following instructions that simulate human's way of thinking.

Computers do not care who gives the instructions. As long as the instructions are loaded into memory, the computer will process it accordingly. Upon startup, a short set of instructions will tell the computer to load and launch the operating system or OS. The OS in turn executes startup instructions that it finds. These include preparing the input and output drivers, as well as launching other background tasks. Having done that, the OS awaits command from its user to execute other applications.

Malware developers take advantage of these key concepts. They find vulnerabilities in the operating and network system that will allow them to install malware and have it running in the background. Vulnerabilities are bugs in the program that can let malware writers load additional code and execute it. These bugs or programming errors do not always appear during the testing stage.

Some malware writers use social engineering to trick victims into installing malware into their computers. They use the computer's connection to internal and external networks to propagate the malware. They infect shared storage to spread malware among colleagues. They hack into servers to install malicious code that will infect site visitors. They can do this because computers will run any executable code that is loaded into its memory.

What is Malware?

Malware is short for malicious software. It is a general term for a code that compromises a computer and instructs it to do malicious tasks, often without the knowledge or permission from the computer's owner. Early malware refers to programming challenges and pranks like programs that delete user files, but recent malware refers to targeting servers to make them inaccessible or for financial gains.

Home computers are not safe, either. Cybercriminals are using home computers to launch attacks on servers in addition to stealing personal information to access online bank accounts. Some advertisers adopt malware, too. They no longer wait for users to visit their sites, but install malware into a victim's computer so they can modify browser settings and change the default home page, eventually advertising their products every time a user opens the browser. They sometimes change the default search engine, replacing it with engines that track user habits to benefit advertisers.

Mobile devices are not safe, either. Today's mobile devices are computers with features and capabilities that are comparable to older computers. Mobile devices, like smartphones and tablets, are vulnerable because they require applications to work. If users inadvertently download a compromised application, then there is a possibility that malware can compromise their mobile devices, too.

A future malware playground is Internet of Things. It is a term for consumer devices like smart home appliances and vehicles loaded with small computers to provide intelligent functionality. These intelligent appliances connect to the Internet for remote control and administration. Having computers on these things, it may not be long until we can see malware on these devices too.

Remember that appliance manufacturers are not IT companies; hence, they may not have the capability to implement data security in their products. A hacker compromising a manufacturer's server could trigger a firmware update on connected appliances and make it perform additional functions, including attacking other servers on the Internet. It may sound like an event from a science-fiction movie, but this reality is possible.

What is the Difference Between a Malware and a Virus?

Many people confuse malware with viruses. A virus is a type of malware, while malware include viruses and other malicious software.

The first malware were viruses, and developers wrote antivirus software to eliminate these malicious programs. Even when viruses evolved to other forms, people still call them viruses and antivirus companies are using the same term even if they are targeting other malware variants.

Viruses are no longer common on their original form. With antivirus vendors constantly updating their algorithms, malware developers have to come up with new variants to avoid detection, often employing social engineering to propagate malware faster by tricking victims to install it along with legitimate software.

If we look at how malware developers remain active over the years, we can surmise that it is a financially rewarding business; therefore, we can expect cybercriminals to continue developing better malware while antivirus companies play catch-up. The only way to combat malware is to understand the threat it presents, how it spreads and propagates, how to detect it, and how to remove.

What are Potentially Unwanted Programs (PUPs)?

People love free software; however, developers need to earn money too. Malware developers see this as an opportunity to spread malware while providing revenue to free-software developers. What they come up with are installers for legitimate software that also install malware during installation. Antivirus companies call these Potentially Unwanted Programs instead of malware since victims give explicit permission to install them. They have no way of knowing if users allow the installation on purpose or unknowingly installs them.

Why would Users Give Permission to Install PUPs?

Most users do not bother reading user agreements that installers display during installation. Instead, they simply click on the default buttons or press enter. Even if users will read the agreements and prompts, some may not understand the message and assume that they are installing software that is necessary for the main program to work. Unfortunately, PUPs are easy to install, but are often frustrating to remove from the system. Most have more than one instance running such that removing a copy will trigger the second copy to re-install it. Many recent PUPs affect users' browsers, which can be very annoying.

How to Detect the Presence of Malware?

Users familiar with their computer will sometimes notice unusual behavior. Some are obvious, like the browser's looks suddenly changing. Other users may lose their files or the file types are changed. Users may even see system errors that were not present before.

Some changes are not visual, like a program accessing the hard disk and making noise even when the computer is idle. Malware accessing an external server can slow down Internet connection. Infected computers can also be unresponsive when hidden processes are running and using up the computer's memory.

Before assuming that malware may be causing the problem, try restarting the computer and leave it for a few minutes without running any program. If the computer is still slow, then there may be an unwanted background program running, but it still needs confirmation.

On Windows, check the hard disk space by opening any folder and clicking Computer on the left. A hard disk with very little space can slow down the computer and malware may not be the cause.

If there is plenty of hard disk space available, run the Task Manager by holding Ctrl+Alt+Del and selecting it from the menu. Click on the Performance tab and observe the real-time graph. Both the CPU and memory usage should be relatively flat if the computer is idle. An active graph could mean that a hidden program is busy. Click the Applications tab to confirm. There should be no application listed if the user did not execute a program. If there is no program listed and the CPU or memory graph is active then there could be a malware running in the background.

To see the process that is using up the memory, click on the Process tab, then click Memory to display the list in descending order. Check its Image name and description. Right-click on a name, then select Properties to get more details. Use a search engine to validate suspicious names.

The Networking tab can also give clues on the presence of malware. There should be no network activity if the computer is idle. If the network is slow and this graph is active, then a hidden program is accessing an external server or computer.

These are just some ways of detecting the possible presence of malware. Without knowing what the malware exactly is; however, it could be difficult to remove it manually.

Most leading antivirus software can detect and remove malware. For home users, there are free versions available that offer basic protection with the option to purchase upgrades for additional features.

A Note on USB flash drives

With the popularity of USB flash drives, spreading malware via USB is easier. Malware can automatically execute when the user opens a USB flash drive. Once in computer memory, inserting another USB drive will infect it. To prevent this, do not view the contents of a USB flash drive after it mounts. Instead, right-click on the drive's name or icon, then select the scan option from the antivirus. This will remove malware in the flash drive before using it.

If there are signs that a USB drive is infected, but the antivirus does not detect it, install another antivirus program. Some antivirus solutions are not good at detecting USB-based malware.

Antivirus solutions can prevent the installation of malware to some extent. However, there are malware that can still get through if the user is not aware of how they propagate. The best way to prevent malware from infecting computers is to understand how each type works.

The succeeding chapters give an insight into the various forms of malware. It also provides information on how they spread so that users can avoid infecting their computers. Prevention is still the best cure against malware. However, avoiding malware is not easy.

Chapter 2 – Virus

Viruses are the earliest forms of malware and they date back to the time before personal computers became popular. A virus is simply a program that can replicate itself on the same computer. Even without malicious intent, creating many copies of a virus code can quickly fill up the memory and slow the computer down. However, an unmodified virus cannot spread to other computers by itself even if the computers are on a network. Getting the virus inside a computer is the challenge for virus creators.

To avoid detection, virus creators modify legitimate programs by inserting malicious codes. When these programs launch, the virus loads into memory and scans the computer for other executable codes to infect. The virus code stays active in memory until the computer shuts down and the cycle starts again if the user runs the infected program.

Boot Sector Virus

Some viruses attack the boot sector of the computer's bootable disks. The boot sector is an area of a disk that a disk drive initially reads and loads into memory. It contains the startup code that will load other components of the operating system. When the boot sector is infected, the virus loads into memory every time the computer starts, ensuring that it is active without waiting for the user to run an infected program. Since the disk operating system can fit in diskettes in the early days of personal computers, starting a clean computer with an infected bootable diskette can also spread the virus to that computer.

Be Careful when Using Shared Resources

Viruses can spread through sharing. When a user mounts a removable storage media on an infected computer while a virus is active, the virus attempts to infect programs that it finds on the mounted media as well. In the early days, this applies to floppy diskettes and external hard drives, but infections are more common today on flash USB drives.

Once the user connects an infected storage to another computer and runs an infected program, the virus activates and infects the other programs in the new computer as well. This makes users who mount USB drives on shared computers at risk if the computer has no sufficient antivirus protection installed. For this reason, avoid connecting USB drives at Internet cafes and on other public computers.

Even shared documents can carry viruses. Some productivity software allows scripts or macros to automate common tasks. Scripts and macros are small, but powerful programs; hence, they can spread viruses, too. Executing an infected macro will also compromise other documents on the same computer. Worse, sending a copy of an infected document can also infect the receiver's computer.

Are Early Viruses Malicious?

Some early viruses started as programming challenges. There was a game that was named Core Wars where the objective is to create a program that loads in memory, then replicate and terminate other programs running on the same memory space. The competing programs create copies of the code while overwriting enemy codes to terminate them. The program that remains in control is the winner.

Other early versions are simply annoying. Two programmers wrote the Brain virus because users were illegally copying their diskettes. The Brain virus simply displays information about the programmers. The Brain virus spread to computers in other countries.

Computers were not widely connected before and the worst thing that a virus can do is to delete files or make them inaccessible. This is exactly what early destructive viruses did. Some programmers wrote viruses that display something interesting while deleting computer files.

Birth of Antivirus Companies

It was not long before other programmers started writing codes to remove viruses, turning the process into a never-ending game of cat and mouse. Virus creators are continually discovering new computer vulnerabilities that they can take advantage of, while antivirus developers update their codes to combat new virus strains. It has become a never ending battle between malware developers and antivirus companies.

Antivirus programs initially identify specific viruses using their signatures. Signatures are like patterns or fingerprints that identify specific viruses. Virus creators responded by continually creating virus variants that require new methods of detection to keep up. This is why antivirus programs update their databases almost daily.

Antivirus can only play catch up if they rely solely on signatures. Modern antivirus programs detect possible viruses by their behavior in addition to signatures.

Most free antivirus software in the market can eliminate common virus threats so not having one installed is not an excuse. While they retain the name, current antivirus software can detect and remove other forms of malware. To enable additional protection, users can purchase additional features.

However, those who do not have a budget for paid features can still protect themselves from malware. The key is to understand how other forms of malware spread. The next chapters will explain these.

11

Chapter 3 - Worms

While viruses were a threat due to their ability to replicate, it is not a tool for mass infection because it cannot spread to other computers. The capability to spread over the network by itself is a feature of worms. Networks include local area networks (LAN) that are commonly found in offices, Wide Area Network (WAN) for remote offices, as well as worldwide networks like the Internet.

Early worm research had good intentions and started as helpful ideas. One worm crawls networked computers at night to run processor-intensive tasks, but saves the work and stays idle during the day so people can use the computers normally. It is a good idea that maximizes computer resources, similar to how modern cloud computing works. However, a programming error caused the computers to crash and they had to write another program to remove it.

Another programmer wrote a seemingly harmless worm to check the size of the Internet. The worm creates copies on target computers as it moved from one computer to the next. Due to a programming decision, it can install a copy even if it already exists on the same computer. Multiple running copies of the same worm can slow down the computer until it eventually crashes. A single worm was able to crash a big part the Internet.

Worms spread across the network by exploiting operating system and application vulnerabilities and taking advantage of insufficient data security practices. Nowadays, worms can also spread through social engineering. Social engineering is a technique used by hackers to trick users into unknowingly breaking standard data security precautions. Hackers can bypass a highly secure environment using social engineering.

Operating systems, or OS, are programs that manage computers and network equipment. Just like any program, it can have unintentional bugs and updating usually fixes the problem. Worms take advantage of these vulnerabilities to compromise the system.

If the OS or application developer releases an update before someone announces the vulnerability, then users have time to update the operating system before a malware exploits the vulnerability. This is why users should install updates especially if the patch is to address data security issues. Allowing automatic updates usually takes care of this, although there is a risk of automatically installing buggy updates.

On the other hand, if a malware creator releases a worm before the developer discovers the bug and releases an update, what we have is zero-day vulnerability. Modern antivirus companies address this by developing algorithms that detect malicious behavior. However, very aggressive antivirus solutions may lead to false positives.

False positives result when a scan reports the presence of malicious code when there is none. A good antivirus has few false positives. Third party evaluations can determine effective antivirus solutions with fewer false positives.

Mass-mailer worms

Worms can access email clients on user computers and use it to email copies of the worm to contacts in the address book. Some of these emails can trick recipients into downloading and installing the attachment, compromising the receiver's computer in the process. When this happens, that computer also becomes a mass-mailing tool. Unfortunately, these worms can also get a name from the address book and change the From field with this name. This means that the sender in the email may not be the email source, making the source difficult to track.

Aside from possibly compromising recipients' computers, mass mailers can also slow down network performance. If a worm infects several computers on the same network, then it could eat up all the allocated bandwidth. Worse, data security companies may include the computer's IP address in the blacklist for spamming. This can affect all computers in the network that shares the same public IP.

This is because most offices and home networks use a single public IP address for their router while individual computers get private IP addresses. Worse, some DSL subscribers may get a banned public IP address when their router restarts.

Always be wary of unsolicited emails with attachment even if it comes from a trusted source. A possible indicator of spam mail is when the receiver's name is not mentioned in the salutation. Bad grammar is also a sign of possible spam email.

Do not assume that the antivirus can catch all worm variants. Some worms change the file extension of the attached file. Users may think that they are opening an image file when in reality they are executing a worm. Worms do this by adding a .jpg to the filename, like picture.jpg.exe. Since many users configure their computers to hide the file extension, they do not see that the real extension is .exe because the filename they see is picture.jpg.

Some mass-mailer worms simply send spam advertisements. While they may not do damage to a user's computer, they can still trick victims into purchasing illegitimate products. These emails often have a web beacon, a small image that is loaded from an external server. Displaying this image will send the user's email address to the server, thereby validating that it is an active email account. It will then be a target for future spam emails.

Note that spammers do not use their own computers to send mass emails. They use email worms to prevent authorities from easily tracking them.

Worms for Phishing

Mass-mailer worms provide a great platform for quickly distributing malware. Malware creators use these worms to transport different payloads depending on their intention. One application of mass-mailers is for phishing.

Phishing is a form of identity fraud and is usually for stealing personal information for financial gains. It works this way.

Malware creators will copy a legitimate website's looks, specifically the login and profile pages. Websites of financial institutions like banks and payment platforms are examples of these. Next, they will create an email that looks like an official document coming from the target institutions. These emails often have a sense of urgency, requiring the user to log in to the website immediately to validate or change the password for security purposes. It will also include a link to the appropriate page for the user's convenience.

There lies the trick. Instead of linking to the legitimate page, it will redirect the user to the fake login page after clicking the email link. The URL will have the legitimate website's domain name, but with added characters. Some users may mistakenly believe that they are in the genuine site and proceed to log in. After entering the login detail, the next page may even require them to enter their credit card details for validation.

In reality, users can enter anything in the login page and it will be successful. The login page will simply save the credentials entered by the user, then display a page to get other credentials. When in doubt, users can initially enter incorrect login credentials to check if the site can really validate their account. If it accepts a wrong username or password, then there is no validation and the site is a fake.

Another way to verify if a website is a fake is through browsing all the menus and internal links before entering the login details. Malware creators may not go through the trouble of recreating an entire website's content.

To guard against phishing, never click on an email link to log in or change account details. Always type the known URL on the browser address bar. If clicking an email link asks the user to log in, then do not continue. Instead, type the correct URL in the browser's address bar before logging in.

The next chapter discusses other payloads that worms usually bring.

Chapter 4 - Trojan Horse

Trojans are malware that disguise as useful programs or install together with a legitimate application. Its name comes from the Trojan War, a part of Greek mythology where a wooden gift horse had soldiers inside that attacked the enemies while they were asleep to win the war. Similarly, a Trojan pretends to be a useful application, waiting for the user to launch it to execute the malicious code. Once activated, trojans will run in the background to do their designated task.

Trojans do not replicate and spread by themselves. They often combine with worms to infect other computers. Trojans are also common on unsolicited email attachments, while some users download them along with valid applications.

There are several types of trojans according to function.

Root kits

Root kit is not inherently bad. It is originally a tool for system administrators. It becomes bad if the creator installs it on a computer without permission from the owner, especially if the purpose is to do malicious tasks.

Some trojans will modify the computer's system for hackers to gain access. Root kits are tools for administrators that hide in the operating system while providing a back door for their creator. With privileged access, a root kit's owner can do almost anything to the infected computer remotely. Root kits are good at hiding their existence, making them difficult to detect. They can also delete any traces of malware installation. Root kits usually remain hidden until activated.

Bots

Bots are programs that perform automated tasks. Some bots, called spambots, flood websites with spam advertisements to generate traffic for another website. This is common in online forums and is the main reason why websites validate users before accepting their registration details. Some registration forms require the user to type the characters shown on an image to validate that the applicant is human. However, some spammers go around this by hiring humans to solve the test, although it comes at a cost.

A more malicious bot is one that employs brute-force attack on target websites. Most website owners do not build websites from scratch, but simply use an open source Content Management System (CMS) as a starting point. A CMS is a fully functioning website that allows the user to update content without writing a single line of HTML code. There are many templates to choose from, and websites owners can customize further by using their own graphic images. Using CMS, owners can update website content in a few clicks.

Many CMS software have the default username "admin" and some website owners do not bother changing it. Given the default administrator name, hackers only need to guess the password to take over the website and install malicious software. If it is a popular forum, then there is a risk that hackers can steal the member database.

To attack a website, hackers write bots that log into the target website and try to log in with passwords taken from a table of common passwords as well as words from the dictionary. A website that does not limit failed logins in a given period is a good target. Using a network of zombie computers, hackers are able to brute-force attack a website using bots with minimal risk of authorities tracking the attack's mastermind.

Stolen password databases from forums are not safe, either. Using rainbow tables, hackers can use brute-force to find the matching password for a member account. Since many users employ the same username and password on all sites they register to, this allows the hackers to hack into members' accounts on other sites as well.

Remote-controlled Bots

Malware developers can turn an infected computer into a remote-controlled bot that will perform malicious tasks, including attacking another computer. This is how they get away with Distributed Denial of Service attacks. Attackers do not use their own computers to flood a server, but instead, they use a large network of zombie computers from unsuspecting users. This also saves the attacker from bandwidth costs since the computer owner is paying for it. It also makes it difficult to track the attacker after it spreads from one computer to another.

One analysis of an affected computer shows that bots log into a chat server, waiting for commands from its master. Think of an army of sleeper bots just waiting patiently for a command to attack. Developers will typically just let an installed Trojan do nothing until they have an army of remote-controlled bots to launch a large-scale cyber-attack. The attacker then issues the command to attack from the chat server where the bots log in each time the infected computer is running.

Without good anti-malware software, the presence of a remote-controlled bot in a computer is difficult to detect since it sleeps until a command is given.

Keylogger

Some trojans can capture keystrokes as well as mouse movements in the background without the user knowing it. Called keyloggers, these programs can serve as surveillance software for a good purpose. Some parents use it to monitor children's online activity.

Trojan keyloggers can steal passwords and other personal credentials from unsuspecting users. It can wait for specific events, like users opening a login page, before starting to record user actions and keystrokes. It then sends the log to a remote server for its master.

Spyware

Spyware is another Trojan that collects sensitive information similar to a keylogger. However, it is not limited to monitoring key strokes to steal user credentials, but can also gather information about the user's online activity as well.

Adware

Adware is similar to spyware, but simply records and sends users' online activity and behavior as marketing data to marketers so they can display an appropriate advertisement. Some versions will redirect browser searches to advertisements while others will replace the default search engine with an advertiser's search engine.

Adware creators write these malware for revenue generation. Adware that alters browser settings is very difficult to remove. Antivirus software can remove adware from the computer, but usually leaves the modified browser settings. Saving browser bookmarks and restoring to factory settings can sometimes fix the problem.

Ransomware

Ransomware does what its name suggests. After installing the malicious code, it will either prevent access to the infected computer or encrypt the contents of its hard disk. Users will see a message demanding payment to disable the malware. The criminals behind typically employ money transfer services that are difficult to track. Add this to the fact that these cybercriminals usually live in other countries, making it difficult to run after them.

To spread ransomware, cybercriminals typically take over a legitimate website, usually without the owner's knowledge, to install the malware. They can also spread ransomware using drive-by downloads on the compromised website.

Drive-by Download

A drive-by download will allow the installation of malware by simply browsing an infected website. The user does not even have to click a download link. The affected website contains codes that check for browser or operating system vulnerabilities that allow for automatic download. The malware will install a program with a task to connect to another server to download the rest of the malware. The victim may not notice the download due to the initial programs' small size.

Some anti-malware software can warn if a website has malware when a user tries to access it.

Suspicious Packers

In order to avoid detection, suspicious packers compress and encrypt malware code. Good anti-malware utilities are aware of this and are able to detect the behavior of suspicious packers and prevent them from executing.

Removing Trojans

Most antivirus companies have software that can automatically remove trojans. While it is possible to remove Trojans manually, this may be a challenge since many have multiple copies running that can reinstall copies if the user deletes one.

When looking for good antivirus software, try the demo versions first. If satisfied, users can pay for other features that provide complete protection to the computer. Some of these protections include email and web surfing security.

In some cases, antivirus software can remove malware from the system, but not from the browser. If removing browser add-ons and restoring to factory setting does not work, uninstall the browser and download again.

Avoiding Installer Trojans

Among the popular sources of Trojans are free software installers. Software development costs money, and offering it free is not good for business. However, many people would prefer free over paid versions, especially when performing simple or one-time tasks. To address this, developers break down their programs by specific features, then allow third party marketers to offer them as free downloads in return for revenue to the developer. For example, one utility can convert AVI formats to MP4, while another can convert MP4 to MPG.

How can marketers earn money from offering free downloads? They get revenue by offering their services to advertisers. These marketers create installers for legitimate software, then include the option to install software from other companies. There is nothing wrong with that right, except that many users do not bother reading what they are installing. Unfortunately, many of these optional programs are adware that antivirus software tag as Potential Unwanted Programs (PUP).

An installer for free software will first confirm that users want to install the desired legitimate program. After the user clicks on the Continue or Next button, the installer will get the user's consent to install additional software along with a few descriptions of its benefits. Sometimes, the installer will display an End User License Agreement (EULA), something that no one ever reads, but simply agrees to. It is common to see more than one program added in the installation. The problem, however, is that the default buttons will install these extra programs if the user is not careful.

How can users avoid these additional installations, especially if the user is unsure if the other software is required? Most installers have a Decline button for optional installations. When an installer shows the Decline button, then that additional software is probably a PUP. Pay attention to the presence of Decline buttons.

Some installers have no separate dialog boxes for additional software installation. Instead, easy and custom install options are available, with the easy install as the default. What the user may not see is that the easy install option will sometimes install additional software. Click the custom install option when it is available and deselect unfamiliar applications.

Some antivirus may give an alert that the installer has a Trojan. Always scan the installer after downloading. Users can do this by selecting the installer, right clicking then selecting the Scan option to run the antivirus. This is also a good practice after inserting USB devices.

Users can perform additional verification after each installation. In Windows, simply select Programs and Features from the control panel, then click the Installed On tab. Sort the list in descending order. The programs with the current date are the ones included in the installation. Select suspicious programs and click uninstall. To verify applications, enter the program name in a search engine to see what it does.

Chapter 5 – Threats on Mobile Devices

Mobile technology is now a part of people's everyday lives. Smartphones today are very powerful. They are no longer just for voice and text, but for accessing the Internet and playing games as well. Though not as efficient as personal computers, users can perform most tasks on their smartphones.

For those who require laptop capability at more portable form factor, tablets are a blessing. Those who want the small size of a phone, but with a bigger screen like a tablet, can choose a phablet. Mobile computing is now a reality.

As computers, these mobile devices can be targets of malware. To minimize these, Android and IOS, the leading mobile platforms, have screening policies in place to reduce the chances of malware getting into the official stores. Additionally, updates to the operating system often include security fixes for known vulnerabilities to strengthen the security of devices. Installing the latest updates, when available to the user's mobile device, addresses possible malware problems.

By default, users can only download apps from the official stores. This is Google Play for Android and App Store for IOS. However, a checkbox on Android's setting will allow the user to download from any external server. There lies the problem.

The price for mobile apps is quite low compared to their PC counterparts. However, many users still do not wish to pay for the apps they download, despite their low prices. Malware creators take advantage of this by making commercial apps available for free download on third party servers. By simply deselecting a default Android setting, users can now download a paid app for free.

Unfortunately, for them, these modified apps may contain malware written for mobile devices. Once installed on a mobile device and executed, these malware take over the device and do what PC malware often do. Some malware may steal user credentials while others may display unwanted advertisements. These malware can make the devices very slow, rendering them unusable. Restoring to factory settings may be the only option for some.

IOS has no checkbox to allow downloading of apps from unofficial sites, but bugs in the operating systems can allow jailbreaks. Jailbreaks are IOS hacks that allow users to customize their devices. It also allows users to install unofficial apps. Some of these apps may have malware and can compromise the device.

Malware creators are smart and can always find ways around a secure system. One company created a Windows application that allows users to download apps for free then transfer them to their IOS device. This comes with a risk, however, since some of these apps may also have malware.

Malware creators started targeting IOS developers in China. They did this by making local copies of Apple's development platform since downloading from Apple's official servers is quite slow for developers located in China. Unfortunately, the unofficial installer has malware that infects the apps they are developing. Some of these apps made their way into the App Store before they were discovered and removed.

Another malware creator took advantage of enterprise certificates. These certificates are used by companies to install their own apps on IOS devices without approval from Apple. Malware creators are tricking users to install an enterprise certificate so they can install apps with malware on victims' devices. Many users who do not understand the implications are at risk.

Apple quickly released an update to IOS that prevents this malware from installing. Those who are still using an older version of IOS can also avoid this malware by not allowing the installation of certificates unless it is from their company's IT department.

For IOS users, downloading apps only from the App Store can minimize the risk of malware. It does not mean that Android users are safer, though. Malware writers are invading Google Play by creating fake apps that mimic original apps, but with additional malware. Google has to monitor millions of apps and ensuring that apps do not have malware is not easy. There is a way to avoid potential malware, though. If an Android app asks for unnecessary permissions during installation, do not install it.

Fortunately, antivirus companies now have versions for both the IOS and Android platforms. Installing these apps will help users screen potential malware during installation, as well as remove malware that were accidentally installed.

Conclusion

Thank you again for purchasing this book!

I hope this book was able to help you understand malware threats to prevent them from spreading.

The next step is to check your computers for signs of malware and apply the lessons in this book to avoid infections in the future.

Finally, if you enjoyed this book, please take the time to share your thoughts and post a review on Amazon. It'd be greatly appreciated!

Thank you and good luck!

Book 2
Robotics
By Kenneth Fraser

The Beginner's Guide to Robotic Building, Technology, Mechanics, and Processes!

Robotics: The Beginner's Guide to Robotic Building, Technology, Mechanics, and Processes!

Robotics: The Beginner's Guide to Robotic Building, Technology, Mechanics, and Processes!

Table of Contents

Introduction

I want to thank you and congratulate you for purchasing the book, *"Robotics: The Beginner's Guide to Robotic Building"*.

This book contains proven steps and strategies on how to build your own robot that will perform certain functions as you want it to do.

For most people, a robot is a machine that could mimic a human such as R2D2 and C3PO in Star Wars. But these types of robots are still in the figments of our imaginations. We are still far from giving robots high level of artificial intelligence to easily adapt and interact to its environment. There is however pioneering works on artificial intelligence that hopes to create humanoid robots.

The type of robots that exist and working today are robots that are programmed to do things that are too dangerous for humans, too repetitive, or just plain messy. These robots are often found in wide range of industries and places such as oil refineries, hospitals, laboratories, factories, and even in the Outer Space. There are about more than a million robots are working in different fields today.

There are types of robots that bring joy to kids such as the popular AIBO ERS-220 that is a bestseller toy during Christmas. While some robots perform great feats by discovering new places and gathering important data in the name of science, specialized robots such as the Mars Rover Sojourner and the underwater robot Caribou are sent to places that average humans cannot go.

Robots are exciting machines to play with, but they are more exciting to build. For hobbyists, building their own robots that capable of doing whatever they program these machines to do gives them pure delight.

This book introduces you to the science of robotics – its basic elements and fundamental concepts. And at the course of your reading, you will learn all the essential aspects you need to build your own robot.

Thanks again for purchasing this book, I hope you enjoy it!

Chapter 1 – What is a Robot?

It is interesting to know that even with all the hype about robots and with all the milestones in robotics, there is still not standard definition for a robot. There are, however, some basic characteristics that a robot should have and this could help you determine if a certain object is a robot or not. It will also guide you in deciding what features you need to build into a machine before you can say that it is a robot.

Four Basic Characteristics of a Robot

A robot has four basic characteristics: sensing, movement, intelligence, and energy.

Sensing

Basically, a robot must be capable of sensing its environment much similar to the way humans sense its surroundings. Robots could either sense through light sensors that mimic the functions of the eyes, or be equipped with chemical sensors that function like the nose, sonar sensors like the nose, touch sensors like the skin, and taste sensors like the tongue. These sensors will help the robot to become aware and understand its environment.

Movement

A robot should have the ability to move around through walking on legs, rolling on wheels, or through propellers. It's either the entire robot is able to move or just some parts of it such as head, arms, or just legs.

Intelligence

A robot should be equipped with artificial intelligence or AI. This is usually done through computer programing. Hence, you need a background in programming to provide your robot with the needed intelligence. You need to program the robot's intelligence so that it will know what to sense and how to move.

Energy

A robot should have a way to power itself. The energy source could be electrical, chemical (battery), or solar. The method by which your robot energizes itself depends on what your robot is required to do.

Working Definition of a Robot

For the purpose of discussion and for reference, we define robot as a machine that contains control systems, sensors, manipulators, software and power supplies that works together to do certain tasks.

Building a robot requires understanding of the fundamental principles of mechanical engineering, mathematics, physics, and computer programming. In special cases, it also requires specific knowledge on chemistry, biology, and medicine. In studying robotics, you need to be actively engaged with wide range of disciplines to build robots that could solve certain problems.

A Brief History of Robotics

The word "robot" was first used in a play entitled R.U.R (Rossum's Universal Robots) written in 1921 by Czech writer Karl Capek. This play is about machines that are built to work on a factory and eventually revolted against their human masters. Robots are the Czech word for slave.

Meanwhile, the word robotics also first appeared in a work of fiction. Russian-born American fictionist Isaac Asimov used it in his short story "Runabout" (1942). Compared to Capek, Asimov had a more positive opinion of the role of robots in the society. In general, he described robots as useful machines that serve humans and perceived them as a "better, cleaner race. He also proposed the three Laws of Robotics:

First Law of Robotics

A robot may not injure a human or, through inaction, allow a human to come to harm.

Second Law of Robotics

A robot must obey the orders given by humans except if such orders would violate the First Law.

Third Law of Robotics

A robot may protect itself as long as such protection do not violate with the First Law or Second Law of Robotics.

Early Models of Robots

Among the earliest cases of a mechanical system designed to perform a regular task was recorded around 3000 BCE. Egyptian water clocks are added with human statuettes to hit the hour bells and signal the passing of time. In 400 BCE,

Robotics: The Beginner's Guide to Robotic Building, Technology, Mechanics, and Processes!

Archytus of Taremtum, who was known as the inventor of pulley and screw, created a pigeon made of wood that is capable of flying. Meanwhile, hydraulically-powered figurines that could speak prophecies were common during the Greek domination of Egypt during the second century BCE.

In the first century C.E., Petronius Arbiter built a doll that is capable of moving like a human being. In 1557, Giovanni Torriani built a wooden robot, which could fetch the Emperor's bread every day from the store. By 1700s, robotic inventions became common with numerous impractical yet ingenious machines such as steam-powered automata crafted in Canada as well as the popular talking doll by Thomas Edison. Even though these creations may have inspired the design and functions for the modern robot, the progress during the 20th century in the field of robotics exceeded previous advancements many times over.

The First Modern Robots

The robots that we are familiar with were built by George C. Devol in the 1950s. The inventor from Kentucky designed and patented a reprogrammable manipulator that he dubbed as "Unimate" derived from "Universal Automation." For years, he tried commercializing his product, but failed. But in 1960s, the entrepreneur-engineer Joseph Englberger bought the patent from Devol and modified it into an industrial robot. He established his company, Unimation, for production and marketing of these products. He was successful in this venture, and in fact, Englberger is regarded today as the Father of Robotics.

Robotics also progressed within the academic institutions. Alan Turing, pioneering computer scientist, mathematician, logician, and cryptologist, published his book "Computing Machiner and Intelligence" where he proposed a test to determine if a machine has the capacity to think for itself. This test is known as the Turing Test.

In 1958, Charles Rosen of the Stanford Research Institute created a research team to work in the development or a robot known as "Shakey" that was more advanced compared to Devol's Unimate. Shakey can move around through the room, sense light through his "eyes" move around strange environment, and to a particular degree, and react to what is happening to his surroundings. He was called Shakey because of his clattering and rickety motions.

In 1966 at Massachusetts Institute of Technology (MIT), Joseph Weizenbaum created an artificial program named ELIZA, which functions as a computer psychologist that manipulates its user's statements to formulate questions.

In 1967, Richard Greenblatt developed MacHack, a program that is capable of playing chess, as a response to a critical article written by Hubert Dreyfuss where he boasted that no computer program can beat him in chess. When the program is finished, Dreyfuss was invited to play and was defeated. This program was the foundation of future chess programs that eventually developed into Big Blue, the program that defeated Grand Master Gary Kasparov in 1997.

The interest in robotics is one of the major catalysts in the development of computers. In 1964, the IBM 360 becomes the first computer to be produced massively.

Robots are also crucial in pioneering space explorations. In 1969, the United States successfully used the latest technology in robotics and computing for Neil Armstrong's landing on the moon. Robots also helped in the expansion of scientific knowledge. In 1994, Carnegie Universities crafted Dante II, an eight-legged walking robot that successfully descends into the crater of Mt Spur to gather samples of volcanic gas.

Commercial companies also leveraged on the mass appeal of robots. In 1999, Sony released its original version of AIBO, a robotic dog that can entertain, learn, and communicate with its owner. Advanced versions have followed in the succeeding years, with the final model, the ERS-7M3, released in 2005.

Honda also released its ASIMO robot, an advanced humanoid robot in 2000. In 2004, Epsom was hailed as the world's smallest robot (7 cm high and weighs only 10 g.) The robotic helicopter is designed to fly and capture videos during natural disasters.

After being released in 2002, a robotic vacuum cleaner known as the Roomba became a huge hit. It sold more than 2.5 million units, which shows that there's really a huge demand for domestic robot technology.

Hundreds of films feature robots such as The Day the Earth Stood Still (1951), Arthur C. Clark's 2001: A Space Odyssey (1968), Star Wars (1977), Blade Runner (1982), Terminator (1984), Nemesis (1992), I, Robot (2004), Transformers (2007), and many more. The popularity of robotic films shows that people are inspired and delighted by the idea of machines that can independently move and think for itself.

If you are ready to build your own robot, continue to the next Chapter to help you get started.

Chapter 2 – Get Started

The first step in building your own robot is to determine what it should do, that is, your purpose of why you are building the robot. Robots can be used in different situations and are mainly designed to assist humans. It will help you a lot to learn first the different purposes and uses of robots.

Basically, robots are divided into two main groups: industrial and domestic robots.

Industrial Robots

Industrial robots are used in factories to manufacture products with precisions such as computers, cars, cellphones, medicine, and even food. Robots increased the productivity in different workplaces, which resulted to booming industries. Each type of industrial robot has its specific form that corresponds to its function. For instance, robotic arms are often used in car assembly lines to spray paint or weld frames. Robotic arms are among the most common robots today. Recently, agricultural robots have been introduced mainly to perform farm tasks such as cutting weeds and harvesting crops.

Domestic Robots

Domestic robots are mainly used in the home to perform household chores. They usually perform repetitive tasks every day such as vacuuming floors, mowing the lawn, vacuuming floors, and other chores that people usually don't have time to do. For example, there are vacuum robots that can clean the floors. They are equipped with motion sensors so they will not run into any object. You just need to push the switch on and it will do its job. It could pick up dust and pet hairs and could be used for hours.

There are also mower robots that could mow lawns. They are equipped with sensors to detect grass edges. Domestic robots are also used for entertainment such as Robosapien, AIBO, and iDog.

Choosing a Robotic Platform

The next step in building your own robot is to decide on the type of robot you want to build. A usual robot design usually begins with "inspiration" of what the robot will do and what it will look like.

The types of robots that you can build are endless. As long as you can envision something that a robot can do, you can work your way to achieve it. But for beginners, you can start with the following types: land robots, aerial robots, aquatic robots, stationary robots, and hybrid robots.

Land Robots

Land-based robots, particularly those added with wheels are among the most common mobile robots built by beginners, because they often require minimal investment while providing the opportunity to learn more about robotics. Meanwhile, the most advanced type of robot is the humanoid robot, which is akin to humans. Humanoids require several degrees of freedom and synchronization of different motors and use several sensors.

Wheeled Robots

Wheels are among the most common method of adding mobility to a robot and are used to mobilize many different sizes of robots and robotic platforms. Wheels could be about any size, and there's no limit in the number of wheels that you can add. More often than not, robots that are equipped with three wheels are using two wheels and a caster at one end. More advanced robots with two wheels are using gyroscopic stabilizing technology.

Meanwhile, robots that are added with four to six wheels usually use several drive motors that decreases the risk of slippage. Also, mecanum wheels or omni-directional wheels can provide the robot considerable benefits in mobility. Most beginners in robotic building are mistaken in thinking that inexpensive DC motors can mobilize robots that are medium in size. As you will learn later, there are more factors that you need to consider before you can add mobility to your robot.

Advantages

Wheeled robots are ideal for beginners as they are often more affordable to build. They have simple design and construction, and there are unlimited options. In addition, robots with six wheels or more could rival the mobility of a track system.

Disadvantages

Wheeled robots usually have small contact area, because only a small portion of the wheel is touching the ground. This results to lower traction that may cause slippage.

Tracked Robots

Tracks are used in tanks for mobility. Even though tracks, also known as treads, don't provide the added torque, they can decrease slippage and can equally distribute the robot's weight. This makes the robot easier to mobilize in loose ground such as gravel and sand. In addition, flexible track systems could easily navigate through a bumpy surface. Most hobbyists also believe that tank tracks are quite cool compared to wheels.

Advantages

Steady contact with the ground avoids slippage, which is prevalent with wheels. The track system also distributes weight evenly, which helps the robot in navigating different surfaces. Tracks can also be used to extensively enhance the ground clearance of the robot without adding a bigger drive wheel.

Disadvantages

The main disadvantage of using a track system for robots is that in turning, there's the tendency to cause damage to the surface that also causes damage to the tracks. In addition, robots are often built around the tracks, and there's a limit in the availability of the tracks. Drive sprocket can also considerably restrict the number of motors that you can use.

Legged Robots

More and more robots are using legs for movement. Legs are usually ideal to use for robots that should navigate on uneven ground. Many prototype robots are built with six legs that allow the robot for static balance. Robots with fewer legs are more difficult to balance as it requires dynamic stability. Once the robot ceases moving in the middle of the stride, it could fall over. Even though there were robots with one leg moving by hopping, bipeds, quadrupeds, and hexapods are the most common forms.

Advantages

The leg motion is the most natural among the platforms, and it can easily overcome big obstacles and move through rough surface.

Disadvantages

Most beginners are discouraged in building their first robot that moves using legs, as it requires high level of electronic, mechanical and coding skills. You also need to find a small battery that can provide the required power, so legged robots are usually expensive to build.

Aerial Robots

Humans have long been inspired by the idea of flight, and this transcends into the field of robotics. The idea of Autonomous Unmanned Aerial Vehicle (AUAV) has gained popularity over the years, and many enthusiasts have developed numerous prototypes. However, the benefits of crafting aerial robots have yet to prevail over the disadvantages. In building aerial robots, many hobbyists are still using commercial remote controllers. Professional aircrafts such as the Predator commissioned by the US military were partially autonomous though recently, updated versions of the Predator have completed aerial missions with only minimum human intervention.

Advantages

Aerial robots are great for surveillance, and remote controlled aircraft has been developed through the years, so there is a diverse community for mechanics where you can find support and know-how in building your own aerial robots.

Disadvantages

There is still limited community when it comes to autonomous control, as most of the knowledge on this field is protected by the US military. Meanwhile, this robot type is expensive as the whole robot could be broken if you miscalculate the steps and lead the robot into a crash.

Aquatic Robots

Recently, more and more hobbyists, communities, and companies are building unnamed aquatic vehicles. There are still many hindrances to overcome in order to make aquatic robots more enticing for the wider communities in robotics. But it is interesting to take note that there are companies today who are manufacturing robots that can clean pools. Aquatic robots can use thrusters, ballast, wings, tails, and fins to move under water.

Advantages

A massive part of the ocean is still unexplored so there's a lot to discover if you choose to build aquatic robots that could help in discovering the underwater world. The robot design is also guaranteed to be unique, and it could be tested in a pool.

Disadvantages

Aquatic robots are often very expensive to build, and there is the risk that the robot could be lost while deep in the ocean. You should also take note that most electronic parts don't pair well with water, especially salty water. You also need to consider the water pressure as going beyond deep sea needs considerable investment and research. There is also very limited robotic community that can provide support, and also limited wireless communication options.

Hybrid Robots

Your concept for the robot may not easily fall into any of the categories mentioned above or could be composed of various functional components. Take note that this book is written to guide you in building mobile robots and not those with fixed designs. In building a hybrid design, it is best to use a modular design where each functional component could be taken off and tested as a separate part.

Advantages

Hybrid robots are designed and built according to your preferences and needs. These robots could be used for various tasks and can be composed of modules. Hybrid robots could lead to versatility and increased functionality.

Disadvantages

Hybrid robots are often complicated to build and expensive. Parts need to be customized to fit the design.

Grippers and Arms

Even though grippers and arms don't fall under the category of mobile robots, robotics basically began with end-effectors and arms. Grippers and arms are the most ideal way for a robot to interact with the environment it is dealing with. Basic robotic arms could have just two to three motions; while more advanced arms could have more than a dozen movements.

Advantages

Most robotic arms and grippers have simple designs, and it is easy to make a three to four degree of freedom robotic arm with a turning base and two joints.

Disadvantages

Robotic arms are stationary unless you fix them on a mobile platform. The cost of building arms or grippers depends on the lifting capacity you need.

In the next chapter, you will learn how to choose the right actuators or motors for your robot.

Chapter 3 – Understanding Actuators

After learning general information about robots and robotics in the first two chapters, it is now time to choose the right actuators to mobilize your robot.

What Are Actuators?

Actuators are devices that transform energy into physical motion. In robotics, this energy is usually electrical energy. Most actuators today produce either linear or rotational motion. For example, a DC motor is a type of actuator.

Selecting the right actuator for your robot requires learning the available actuators, and some fundamental knowledge of physics and mathematics.

Rotational Actuators

Rotational actuators convert electrical energy into rotating motion. There are two primary mechanical parameters that distinguish each actuator: (a) the rotational speed that is often measured in revolutions per minute or rpm and (b) torque or the force that the devices can produce at a given distance often expressed in Oz•in or N•m.

AC Motor

Alternating Current (AC) is rarely used in robots because most of them are powered through Direct Current (DC) in form of cells or batteries. In addition, electronic parts use DC, so it is easier to use the same type of power supply for the actuators. AC motors are primary used in industrial settings where high torque is necessary or where the motors are connected to a wall outlet.

DC Motor

DC motors are often cylindrical in shape but they also come in different shapes and sizes. They also have output shafts that rotate at high speed often between 5000 and 10000 rpm. Even though DC motors rotate very fast, most have low torque. To decrease the speed and add torque, a gear could be added. To install a motor into a robot, you must fix the body of the motor to the robot's frame. Hence, motors usually have mounting holes that are basically located on the motor's face so that they can be easily installed. DC motors could either rotate in counter clockwise or clockwise. The angular movement of the turning shaft could be measured using potentiometers and encoders.

Geared DC Motor

A DC Motor could be added with a gearbox to reduce the motor's speed and enhance its torque. For instance, if a DC motor rotates at 5000 rpm and produces a 0.0005 N•m of torque, adding a 123:1 ("one hundred and twenty three to one") gear would reduce the speed by a factor of 123 (resulting to 5000 rpm / 123 = 40 rpm) and increase the torque by a factor of 123 (0.0005 x 123 = 0.0615 N•m). The most common types of gears are planetary, spur, and worm. Similar to a DC motor, a geared DC motor can also rotate in either clockwise or counter clockwise. You can add an encoder to the shaft if you want to know the number of rotations of the motor.

Hobby Servo Motors

Hobby Servo Motors, also known as R/C Servo Motors are actuators that rotate to a certain angular position, and were traditionally used in more expensive remote controlled machines for controlling or steering flight surfaces. Today, they are used in different applications so their prices have been reduced considerably, and the variety has also increased. Most servo motors can only rotate about 180 degrees. A hobby servo motor is composed of a DC motor, electronics, gears, and a potentiometer that measures the angle. The latter works with the electronics to mobilize the motor and stop the output shaft at a certain angle. In general, these servos have three wires, voltage in, control pulse, and ground. A robot servo is a recently developed servo that provides both position feedback and continuous rotation. Servos could rotate clockwise or counterclockwise.

Stepper Motors

As the name implies, stepper motors rotates following certain steps or degrees. The number of degrees the shaft rotates with every step could vary depending on various factors. Majority of stepper motors don't include gears, so similar to a DC motor, the torque is quote low. Fixing gears to a stepper motor has similar effect as installing gears to a DC motor.

Linear Actuators

Linear actuators produce linear movements. They have three primary distinctive mechanical properties: (a) the force measured in kg or lbs (b) speed measured in m/s or inch/s and (c) the maximum and minimum distance that the rod could move also known as the stroke measured in inches or mm.

Linear DC Actuator

A linear DC actuator is usually composed of a DC motor attached to a lead screw, which also turns as the motor moves. The lead screw has a traveler that is forced either away or towards the motor, basically transforming the rotating motion to a linear movement. Some DC linear actuators integrate a linear potentiometer that adds a linear position feedback.

Solenoids

Solenoids are comprised of a coil wound surrounding the mobile core. Once the coil is energized, the core is forced away from the magnetic field and creates a motion in one direction. Several coils or some mechanical arrangements will be needed to provide movements in different directions. A solenoid stroke is often very small but they are often very fast. The strength primarily depends on the size of the coil and the electrical power passing through it.

Hydraulic and Pneumatic Actuators

Hydraulic and pneumatic actuators use liquid or air respectively to create a linear movement. These actuators could have lengthy strokes, high speed and high force. To use these actuators, you need to use a fluid or air compressor that makes them harder to use compared to basic electrical actuators. These are often used in industrial applications because of their large size and high force speed.

Muscle Wire

Muscle wire is a specialized wire, which contracts when electricity passes through it. When electricity is gone and once the wire cools down, it will go back to its original length. This type of actuator is not fast, strong, or creates a long stroke. Nonetheless, it is one of the most convenient actuators to use if you need to work with smaller parts.

How to Choose the Proper Actuator for Your Robot

To guide you in choosing the actuator for certain tasks, consider answering the following questions to help you.

Take note that new innovations and technologies are always being released regularly, so nothing is permanent. Also remember that one actuator could perform various tasks in various contexts.

1. Do you need to mobilize a wheeled robot?

Drive motors should carry the weight of the whole robot and will most likely need a gear down. Majority of the robots utilize "skid steering" while trucks or cars utilize rack and pinion steering. If you prefer the skid steering, geared DC motors are recommended to use for robots with tracks or wheels. Geared motors provide constant rotation, and could have discretionary position feedback through optical encoders. Because the rotation needed is limited to a certain angle, you can choose a hobby servo motor for stirring.

2. Is there a limit on the range of motion?

If the range is restricted to 180 degrees and the needed torque is not a critical factor, a hobby servo motor is recommended. Servo motors are available in various torques and sizes and comes with angular position feedback. Majority of these motors use potentiometer, while some specialized ones use optical encoders. R/C servos are now popularly used to build small walking robots.

3. Do you need a motor to lift or turn heavy loads?

Raising a weight needs considerably more power compare to moving a weight on a flat surface. Torque should be prioritized than the speed, and it is ideal to use a gearbox with a powerful DC motor or a linear DC actuator with a high gear ratio. You can use an actuator system that could prevent the mass from falling if there is a disruption in the power source. This includes clamps or worm gears.

4. Do you need the angle to be precise?

Stepper motors that are paired with a motor controller cold provide a very precise angular motion. They are more ideal to use compared to servo motors because they provide constant rotation. But there are also high-end digital servo motors that use optical encoders and can provide high precision.

5. Do you need to achieve movements in a straight line?

Linear actuators are ideal for moving parts and placing them in a straight line. They are available in different configurations and sizes. For fast movements, you must consider solenoids or pneumatics, for high torques, you can use linear DC actuators or hydraulics, and if the movement requires minimum torque, you can use muscle wire.

Chapter 4 - Microcontrollers and Motor Controllers

Microcontrollers are considered as the "brain" of the robot because it is responsible for all decision making, computations, and communications. These are devices with the capacity to execute a program (a series of instructions).

To interact with the external world, a microcontroller has a sequence of electrical signal connections (known as pins), which could be switched on or off using programming functions. These pins are also used in reading electronic signals that are released by sensors or other devices and determine if they are low or high.

Majority of microcontrollers today could measure analogue voltage signals, or signals that could have a full range of values rather than just two specified states by using analog to digital converter or ADC. Through the use of ADC, a microcontroller could assign a numerical value to the analog voltage that is neither low nor high.

What Could Microcontrollers Do?

Numerous complicated actions could be achieved by setting the pins low and high creatively. Nonetheless, building complicated algorithms such as smart movements and data processing or complicated programs are not yet on the range of microcontrollers because of its natural speed and resource limitations.

For example, to light a blinker, you can program a repeating sequence in which the microcontrollers could turn a pin high, wait for several seconds, turn it low, wait for several seconds and goes back to the first sequence. A light that is connected to the pin will then blink open-endedly.

Similarly, microcontrollers could be used to take control of other electronic devices including actuators when they are installed to motor controllers, Bluetooth or WiFi interfaces, storage devices, and many more. Because of its versatility, microcontrollers could be found in common everyday products. Basically, every home electrical device or home appliance utilizes at least one microcontroller.

Not similar to microprocessors found in Central Processing Units in personal computers, microcontrollers don't need peripherals such as external storage devices or external RAM to operate. Hence, even if the microcontrollers are less powerful compared to microprocessors, building circuits and products based on microcontrollers is an easier task and a lot more affordable, because minimal hardware parts are needed. Remember, microcontrollers can output minimum amount of electrical power through pins. Hence, a generic microcontroller cannot power solenoids, power electrical motors, large lights, or other direct loads. Doing this could cause physical damage to the controller.

Programming Microcontrollers

There's no need to shy away from programming microcontrollers. Not similar in the past where making a blinker took comprehensive knowledge of microcontroller and at least a dozen line of code, programming microcontrollers is fairly easy today. You can use the simplified Integrated Development Environments (IDE), which uses modern languages, full line archives that could cover all of the most common actions, and several handy samples to help you get started. You can learn more about programming your robot in Chapter 6.

How to Choose the Proper Microcontroller for Your Robot

You will need a microcontroller for any robotic building project unless you're into BEAM robotics or you want to control your robot through an R/C system or a tether. For starters, selecting the right microcontroller could seem like a difficult job, particularly considering the product range, specifications, and applications. There are various microcontrollers available today such as BasicATOM, POB Technology, Pololu, Arduino, BasicX, and Parallax.

The following questions could guide you in choosing the right microcontroller:

1. Which microcontroller is widely used for your type of robotic project?

Building robots is not a popularity contest, but the fact that a microcontroller has a large supporting community or has been used in the same project can make the design phase easily. With this, you can benefit from other experience and hobbyists. It is common for hobbyists to share codes, pictures, instructions, and videos even lessons learned.

2. Do you need specific accessories for a certain microcontroller?

If your robot has special needs or there is a certain accessory or component that is important for your design, selecting a compatible microcontroller is clearly essential. Even though most accessories and sensors could be directly interfaced with most microcontrollers, some accessories are designed to interface with a particular microcontroller.

3. Do you need special features for your robot?

A microcontroller should be able to perform all the special actions needed for your robot to function well. Some features are common to all microcontrollers such as being able to execute basic mathematical operations, having digital inputs and outputs, and making decisions. Others may need certain hardware such as PWM, ADC, and communication protocol support. You must also consider pin counts, memory and speed requirements

Motor Controllers

Motor controllers are electronic devices that serve an intermediary device between a microcontroller, the motors, and the power supply.

Even though the microcontroller decides the direction and the speed of the motors, it doesn't have enough power to directly drive them. Meanwhile, the motor controller can supply the current at the needed voltage but doesn't have the capacity to decide how fast the motor must turn.

Hence, the microcontroller and the motor controller must work together to make the motors move accordingly. The microcontroller can provide instructions to the motor controller on how to power up the motors through a standard and basic communication method such as PWM and UART. In addition, some motor controllers could be manually regulated using an analog voltage often created through a potentiometer.

The size and weight of a motor controller may greatly vary from a device that is smaller than the tip of a pencil to a huge controller that could weight several kilos. The size and weight often has a minimum effect on the robot, unless you want to build unnamed aerial or aquatic robots.

Types of Motor Controllers

Because there are several types of actuators (as we have discussed in Chapter 3), there are also several types of motor controllers: brushed DC motor controllers, brushless DC motor controllers, servo motor controllers, and stepper motor controllers.

How to Choose a Motor Controller

You can only choose a motor controller after you have decided on what type of actuator you want to use. In addition, the current that a motor draws depends on the torque it could provide. A small DC motor will not use much current, but cannot also release much torque, while a bigger motor could release higher torque but will need increased current.

Chapter 5 - Controlling Your Robot and Use of Sensors

Based on our definition of a robot, it should gather data about its surroundings, make smart decisions and then execute actions based on calculations. This also includes the option for the robot to become semi-autonomous (with aspect that are controlled by humans and other aspects that it can do on its own).

One good example of this is a complex aquatic robot. A human controls the basic motions of the robot while an installed processor measures and reacts to the underwater currents to keep the robot in one position while still preventing a drift. A camera installed in the robot would send videos back to the human while the sensors could track the water pressure, temperature, and more. Once the communication line falters between the robot and the human, an autonomous program could take over to instruct the robot to reach for the surface.

In controlling your robot, you need to figure out the level of autonomy. You need to choose if you want the robot to be tethered, wireless, or autonomous.

Tethered

Direct Wired Control

The simplest way to control a vehicle is by using a handheld controller that is physically connected to a vehicle using a tether or a cable. Knobs, switches, joysticks, buttons, and levers on the controller will allow you to control the robot without the need to add sophisticated electronics. In this setting, the power source and motors could be directly connected with a switch to control the rotation. These machines often have no artificial intelligence and are regarded as remote controlled devices than robots.

Wired Computer Control

Another method is to integrate a microcontroller into the machine but still using a tether. Attaching the microcontroller to your computer's ports will allow you to control the actions using the keyboard, a joystick, a keypad, or other device. Adding a microcontroller to your robot project may also require programming how the robot will respond to the input.

Ethernet

Another way to use computer control is to use an Ethernet interface. A robot that is directly connected to a router can also be used for mobile robots. Building a robot, which can communicate through the internet could be sophisticated, and usually a wireless internet connection is more recommended.

Wireless

Infrared

You can ditch away cables and wires if you use infrared transmitters and receivers. This is often a great achievement for beginners. Infrared control needs "line of sight" to function. The receiver should have the ability to see the transmitter to receive the data. Infrared remote controls can be used to send commands to infrared receivers that are paired with microcontrollers that interpret these signals and control the actions of the robot.

Radio Frequency

Remote control units often use microcontrollers in the receiver and transmitter for data transmission through radio frequency. The receiver box usually has a printed circuit board (PCB) that includes a small servo motor controller and a receiving unit. RF communication needs a transmitter matched with a receiver or a transceiver. RF doesn't need clear line of sight and could also provide considerable distance. Basic RF devices could allow for data transfer between devices between long distances, and there's no limit to the range for more RF devices.

Bluetooth

Bluetooth is a type of Radio Frequency and follows certain protocols for sending and receiving data. Standard Bluetooth range is usually restricted to about 10 meters although it has the advantage of controlling the robot though Bluetooth-enabled devices including laptops, smartphones, and PDAs. Similar to RF, Bluetooth provides two-way communication.

WiFi

Recent development in wireless technology enables you to control a robot through the Internet. To build a WiFi robot, you must have a wireless router that is connected to the internet and a WiFi device on the robot. You can also use a device, which is enabled with TCP/IP with a wireless router.

Autonomous

High-level robots are autonomous. With recent developments, you can now use the microcontroller in its full potential and program it to respond to input from the sensors. Autonomous control may come in different types: restricted sensor feedback, pre-programmed with no feedback from the environment, and complex sensor feedback. Genuine "autonomous" control includes different sensors and code to allow the robot to figure out by itself the smartest action to be taken in any situation.

The most sophisticated methods of control presently used on autonomous robots are auditory and visual commands. For auditory control, a robot will react to the sound of the human's voice for instructions such as "get the ball" or "turn left." For visual command, a robot may look to an object to decide on what to do. Instructing a robot to turn to the right by showing a drawing of an arrow that is pointing to the right requires complicated programming. Even though these things are no longer impossible, they need a sophisticated level programming and usually hundreds of hours.

Not similar to humans, robots are not restricted to just sound, sight, smell, touch, and taste. Robots use different electromechanical sensors to understand and discover their surroundings. Mimicking a natural organism's senses is presently a great challenge, so developers and robotic builders are using alternatives to these natural senses.

Chapter 6 - Assembling and Programming a Robot

After learning all about the fundamental blocks in building a robot, the next stage is the designing and building of the frame that will keep all the components together and will provide your robot a definite look and shape.

Constructing the Frame

There's no fix method in creating a frame, because there is often a trade-off to be constructed. You may prefer to use a lightweight frame but you may need to use costly materials. You may like a strong or big chassis but you may realize it is expensive, hard, or heavy to produce. The frame could be complicated and may take some time to design and build.

Materials

There are different materials that you can use in creating a frame for your robot. As you try different materials to construct not only robots but other types of machines, you will also understand the advantages and the disadvantages as to which material is the most suitable for a specific project. The roster of suggested building materials below comprises only the more common one, and when you have tried several of these materials, you can start experimenting or blending some together.

Basic Construction Materials

Some of the most basic construction materials could be used to build good-quality frames. The cheapest materials is the cardboard that you can usually find for free and could easily be bent, cut, layered, or bent. You can construct a reinforced cardboard box that looks a lot nicer and is more proportional when it comes to the size of your robot. You can then paint it with glue or epoxy to make it stronger then add extra layer of paint.

Structural Flat Materials

For a more durable frame, you can use a standard structural material such as a sheet of plastic, metal, or wood. You just need to puncture some holes to connect the electronic components. A stronger piece of wood has a tendency to be heavy and thick, while a thin sheet of metal could be too flexible. You can attach components to both sides and the wood will still remain solid and intact.

If you're at the stage where you are ready to have an outsourced frame, the best option is to acquire the part precision cut through a water or laser jet. Hiring a third-party to produce a custom part is recommended only if you are completely sure of the dimensions, because the mistakes could be expensive. Companies that offer computer controlled cutting services may also provide different other services such as painting and bending.

3D Printing

Building a frame constructed from 3D printed panels is not always the most structurally sound option, primarily because it is built up in several layers. However, this process could produce complex and detailed shapes that could be impossible to build using other methods. One 3D printed component may contain all the important mounting points for all mechanical or electrical parts without compromising the robot's weight. In the past decade, the cost of 3D printing is quite expensive, but as it becomes popular, the price of producing the components is also expected to go down.

Assembling the Parts Together

With the available options for materials and methods, you can now start assembling the parts together. You can follow the steps below to build a simple, aesthetic, and structurally reliable robot frame.

1. Decide on the material you want to use.

2. Gather all the parts that your robot will need, both mechanical and electrical and measure them. In case you don't have all the components ready, you can refer to the dimensions that are often supplied by the manufacturers.

3. Think of and draw various designs for your frame. It's fine not to provide details.

4. Once you find the suitable design, be certain that the structure is reliable and all the parts would be supported in the frame.

5. Sketch every component of the robot on cardboard or paper at true scale. You can also draw the parts in the CAD software and print them.

6. Test the design in CAD and in actual setting using your paper prototype by test fitting every component and connection.

7. Measure the dimensions again and when you are completely certain that your design is right, begin cutting the frame into the material. Take note to measure two times and only cut once.

8. Test fit every part before assembling the frame if in case you need some changes.

9. Construct the frame using appropriate assembling materials such as glue, nails, screw, duct tape, or any appropriate binding tools that you prefer.

10. Fit all the parts into the frame and there you go, you have just built your robot!

Constructing the Robot Parts

The last step discussed above should be described further. In the past chapters, you have already chosen the electrical parts including the actuators, microcontroller, and motor controller. The next step is to construct them so they will work together.

In the following section, we'll use standard cable colors and terminal names that encompass common parts. You must rely on manuals and datasheets when you are working on your specific parts.

Attaching Motor Controllers to Motors

A geared DC motor or a linear DC actuator usually has two wires: black and red. Attach the black wire to the M- terminal on the DC motor controller and the red wire to the M+ terminal. Connecting the wires the other way around will only cause the motor to rotate in the opposite direction. Meanwhile, servo motors have three wires: red, black, and yellow. A servo motor controller comes with pins that are matching these wires so you can just plug it directly.

Attaching Microcontroller to Motor Controllers

Microcontrollers can communicate with motor controller in different ways: 12C, R/C, Serial, or PWM. Be sure to refer to the manual for each microcontroller for specific instructions on proper connection. Regardless of the method you choose, the microcontroller and the logic of the motor controller should share matching ground reference. This can be achieved by attaching the GND pins together. Meanwhile, a logic level shifter is needed if the devices don't share the same logic levels.

Attaching Batteries to a Microcontroller or a Motor Controller

Majority of the motor controllers available today have two screw terminals for the battery labels marked with B- and B+. If the batteries you got are provided with a connector and the controller comes with screw terminals, you could still search for a pairing connector with wires that you can attach to the screw terminal. If this is possible, you need to find another way to link the battery to the motor controller while you can still unplug the battery and link it to a charger. It's possible that not all the electrical and mechanical components you have selected for your robot could operate on a single voltage, and so may need several voltage regulation circuits or batteries.

If you are building a robot with a microcontroller, DC gear motors, and maybe servo motors, it's easy to see how a battery may not be able to power every component directly. Nevertheless, it is best to choose a battery that can directly power as many devices that you need. The battery with the largest capacity must be connected with the drive motors. For instance, if the motors you select are rated a nominal 12 volts, the primary battery must also be 12 volts. So you can use a regulator to energize a 5 volts microcontroller. LiPo and NiMH batteries are the top choices for small to medium robots. Select NiMH if you need cheaper batteries and LiPo if you need light weight batteries. Always take note that batteries are powerful devices that could easily burn your circuits if they are not properly connected. Always make sure that the polarity is correct and that your device could handle all the energy supplied by the battery. If you are not certain, never make assumptions.

Adding Electrical Parts to Frame

You can attach electrical components to your frame through different methods. Make certain that whatever method you use, don't conduct electricity. Usual methods include screws, hex spacers, Velcro, double-sided tape, cable ties, glue, and many more.

Programming Your Robot

Programming is often the last step in building your robot. If you have followed the steps described in the previous chapters, by now you have selected the electrical components such as actuators, microcontrollers, motor controllers, sensors, and more. At this point, you might have already constructed your robots and hopefully it looks something like you want it to be. But without the proper program, your robot is just a cool paperweight.

It requires another book to teach you robotic programming. Instead, this section will guide you on how to get started and what you should learn.

There are several programming languages that you can use to program the microcontroller that will serve as the brain of your robot. The following are the most common programming languages you can choose:

Assembly

This programming language is just a shy away from programming a full-pledged computer, and so it could be difficult to use. This language is ideal to use if you really need to ensure complete instruction-level control of your robot.

Basic

Basic is one of the most common programming languages for robot hobbyists. This is often used in programming microcontrollers mainly for educational robots.

C++

C++ is a very popular programming language. It provides top=level functionality while you are keeping a good low-level control. A variant of C++ is Processing, which includes simplified codes to make the programming easier.

Java

Java is more developed compared to C++ and offers any safety features to the disadvantage of low-level control. Some producers of microcontrollers such as Parallax are making components for specific use with Java.

Python

Python is one of the most popular languages for scripting. It is easy to learn and could be used to quickly and efficiently integrate several programs.

If you have selected a hobbyist type of microcontroller from a known producer, there's a chance that you can find a book that you can read so you can learn how to program in their preferred programming language. But if you instead prefer a microcontroller from a smaller producer, it is crucial to see what language the controller wants to use and what tools are available.

Conclusion

Thank you again for purchasing this book!

I hope this book was able to help you to learn the basic building blocks of robot building.

The next step is to expand your knowledge in robotics, especially learning advanced programming for your robot.

Finally, if you enjoyed this book, please take the time to share your thoughts and post a review on Amazon. It'd be greatly appreciated!

Thank you and good luck!

Book 3
Cryptography
By Solis Tech

Cryptography Theory & Practice Made Easy!

Cryptography: Cryptography Theory & Practice Made Easy!

Table of Contents

Introduction

I want to thank you and congratulate you for purchasing the book, *Cryptography*.

This book contains tips and techniques on how to build cryptosystems – even if you're just a complete beginner.

This eBook will help you learn about the history and basic principles of cryptography. It will teach you the different aspects of message encryption. In addition, you will learn how to establish cryptosystems. Aside from discussing modern/digital encryption schemes, this book will teach you how to use different types of "practical" ciphers.

Thanks again for purchasing this book. I hope you enjoy it!

Chapter 1: Cryptography – History and Basic Concepts

The Origin of Cryptography

During the ancient times, people needed to do two things: (1) to share information and (2) protect the information they are sharing. These things forced individuals to "encode" their messages. This "encoding" process protects the message in a way that only the intended recipient can understand the information. That means the data will remain secure even if unauthorized parties get access to it.

The art and science of protecting information is now known as "cryptography." The term "cryptography" was formed by fusing two Greek terms, "Krypto" (which means "hidden") and "graphene" (which means writing).

According to historians, cryptography and "normal" writing were born at the same time. As human civilizations progressed, people organized themselves into groups, clans, and kingdoms. These organizations led to the creation of concepts such as wars, powers, sovereignty, and politics. Obviously, these ideas involve information that cannot be shared with ordinary citizens. The group leaders needed to send and receive information through protected means. Thus, cryptography continued to evolve.

The Contributions of Egyptians and Romans

1. Egyptians

The oldest sample of cryptography can be found in Egypt. Ancient Egyptians used hieroglyphs (i.e. a system of writing that involves symbols and images) to share and record pieces of information. In general, these symbols and images are only intelligible to the priests who transmitted messages on behalf of the pharaohs. Here is a sample hieroglyph:

Fig. 1 - Egyptian Hieroglyphs

Several thousands of years later (around 600 to 500 BC), Egyptian scholars started to use simple substitution codes. This style of encoding involved the replacement and/or combination of two or more alphabets using a secret rule. This rule was considered as the "key" in retrieving the real message from the coded "garbage."

2. Romans

Ancient Romans used a system of cryptography known as the Caesar (or Shift) Cipher. This system depends on moving each letter of the message by a certain number (three is the most popular choice). To decode the information, the recipient simply needs to "move" the letters back using the same number. Here is an example:

Fig. 2 – Caesar Cipher

Cryptography – Fundamental Concepts

Encryption – This is the process of converting information into an unintelligible form. It helps in securing the privacy of the message while it is being sent to the recipient.

Decryption – This process is the exact opposite of encryption. Here, the encoded message is returned to its natural form.

Important Note: Encryption and decryption requires specific rules in converting the data involved. These rules are known as the key. Sometimes, a single key is used to encrypt and decrypt information. However, there are certain scenarios where these two processes require different sets of keys.

Plaintext and Ciphertext – The term plaintext refers to data that can be read and used without the application of special techniques. Ciphertext, on the other hand, refers to data that cannot be read easily: the recipient needs to use certain decryption processes to get the "real" message.

Authentication – This is probably one of the most important aspects of cryptography. Basically, authentication serves as a proof that the information was sent by the party claimed in the encoded message.]

Let's illustrate this concept using a simple example: John sent a message to Jane. However, before replying, Jane wants to make sure that the message really came from John. This verification procedure can be conducted easily if John does "something" on the message that Jane knows only John can do (e.g. writing his signature, including a secret phrase, folding the letter in a certain way, etc.). Obviously, successful decryption of the message will be useless if the information came from an unwanted source.

Integrity – Loss of integrity is one of the biggest problems faced by people who use cryptography. Basically, loss of integrity occurs whenever the message gets altered while it is being sent to the receiver. Unnecessary and/or unwanted modifications in a message may cause misunderstanding and other issues. Because of this, the message must be protected while it is being delivered. Modern cryptographers accomplish this through the use of a cryptographic hash (i.e. a hash function that is extremely difficult to invert, modify, or recreate).

Non-Repudiation – This concept focuses on ensuring that the sender cannot deny that he/she sent the encoded message. In the example given above, it is important to make sure that John cannot deny the fact that he was the one who sent the message. Modern cryptography prevents this "sender repudiation" using digital signatures.

Chapter 2: The Modern Cryptography

For some people, modern cryptography is the foundation of technology and communications security. This type of cryptography is based on mathematical concepts like the number theory, the probability theory, and the computational-complexity theory. To help you understand modern cryptography, here is a comparison of the "classical" and "modern" types of cryptography.

Classical Cryptography

1. It utilizes common characters (e.g. letters and numbers) directly.

2. It relies heavily on the "obscure is secure" principle. The encryption and decryption processes were considered as confidential information. Only the people involved in the communication can access such data.

3. It needs an entire cryptosystem (will be explained in the next chapter) to complete the "confidential" transfer of information.

Modern Cryptography

1. It relies on modern technology like binary data sequences.

2. The information is encoded through the use of mathematical algorithms accessible to the public. Here, security is achieved through a "secret key" which is used as the foundation for the algorithms. Two factors ensure that "outsiders" cannot access the information even if they have the correct algorithm:

   a. It is extremely difficult to compute such algorithms. Thus, it is hard to extract any information from them.

   b. The absence or presence of secret keys.

3. The encryption doesn't involve the entire cryptosystem. Only the interested parties are required to participate in encoding and decoding the message.

Chapter 3: Cryptosystem – The Basics

A cryptosystem is the application of cryptographic methods and their appropriate coding environment (also called "infrastructure"). This system is used to add security to technology and communications services. Some people refer to cryptosystems as "cipher systems."

To illustrate the concept of cryptosystems, let's consider the following example:

Fig. 3 – A Cryptosystem

In this example, the sender encrypts his message (i.e. the plaintext) through the use of a key. This process converts the plaintext into ciphertext. Once the receiver gets the ciphertext, he uses the same key to decrypt the information. Thus, the ciphertext will be turned into plaintext again.

As you can see, only the parties who have the "key" can access the shared information. Cryptosystems can be divided into these basic components:

- Plaintext – The information that needs to be shared and protected.

- Encryption Algorithm – The mathematical process that uses a plaintext and an encryption key to produce a ciphertext.

- Ciphertext – The coded version of the information. In general, cryptography protects the message itself, not the transmission. That means the coded message is sent through public channels such as emails. Thus, anyone who can access the selected delivery channel can intercept or compromise the message.

- Decryption Algorithm – It is a mathematical process that creates plaintext from any given set of ciphertext and decryption key. Basically, it reverses the encryption process done earlier in the transmission of the message.

- Encryption Key – The value provided by the sender. In creating the ciphertext, the sender enters this key (along with the plaintext) into the encryption algorithm.

- Decryption Key – The value known by the recipient. The decryption key is always related to the encryption key used for the message. However, these keys don't have to be identical. The recipient enters the decryption key and the ciphertext into the decryption algorithm in order to get the plaintext. The collection of all decryption keys for a cryptosystem is known as a "key space."

There are times when an interceptor (also called "attacker") tries to get the encoded message. In general, interceptors are unauthorized entities who want to access the ciphertext and determine the information it contains.

The Two Kinds of Cryptosystems

Currently, cryptosystems are divided into two kinds: (1) Symmetric Key Encryption and (2) Asymmetric Key Encryption. This way of classifying cryptosystems is based on the method of encryption/decryption used for the entire system.

The major difference between the symmetric and asymmetric encryptions is the connection between the encryption and decryption keys. Generally speaking, all cryptosystems involve keys that are closely related. It is impossible to create a decryption key that is totally unrelated to the code's encryption key. Let's discuss each kind of cryptosystems in more detail:

Symmetric Key Encryption

Cryptosystems that belong to this kind have a single key. This key is used to encrypt and decrypt the information being sent. The study of symmetric encryption and systems is known as "symmetric cryptography." Some people refer to symmetric cryptosystems as "secret key" systems. The most popular methods of symmetric key encryption are: IDEA, BLOWFISH, DES (Digital Encryption Standard), and 3DES (Triple-DES).

During the 1960s, 100% of the cryptosystems utilized symmetric encryption. This method of encrypting and decrypting information is so reliable and efficient that it is still being used even today. Businesses that specialize on Communications and Information Technology consider symmetric encryption as the best option available. Since this kind of encryption has distinct advantages over the asymmetric one, it will still be used in the future.

Here are the main characteristics of symmetrically encrypted cryptosystems:

- Before transmitting the message, the sender and the receiver must determine the key that will be used.

- The key must be changed regularly to avoid any intrusion into the cryptosystem.

- A stable form of data transmission must be established to facilitate easy sharing of the key between the involved parties. Since the keys must be changed on a regular basis, this mechanism may prove to be expensive and complicated.

- In an organization composed of "x" individuals, to facilitate two-way communication between any two members, the required number of keys for the entire system is derived using the formula: "x * (x-1)/2."

- The keys used are often small (i.e. measured through the number of bits involved), so the encryption and decryption processes are faster and simpler compared to those used for asymmetric systems.

- These cryptosystems do not require high processing capabilities from computer systems. Since the keys used are small and simple, ordinary computers can be used to establish and manage the cryptosystem.

Here are the two problems usually encountered when using this kind of cryptosystem:

- Key Determination – Before any message can be transmitted, the sender and the receiver must determine a specific symmetric key. That means a secure and consistent way of creating keys must be established.

- Trust Issues – Because all the people involved use the same key, symmetric key cryptography requires the sender to trust the receiver, and vice versa. For instance, if one of them shares the key with an unauthorized party, the security of the entire cryptosystem will be ruined.

Modern day communicators say that these two concerns are extremely challenging. Nowadays, people are required to exchange valuable data with non-trusted and non-familiar parties (e.g. seller and buyer relationships). Because of these problems, cryptographers had to develop a new encryption scheme: the asymmetric key encryption.

Asymmetric Key Encryption

These cryptosystems use different keys for encrypting and decrypting the message. Although the keys involved are dissimilar, they still have a logical and/or mathematical relationship. It is impossible to extract the message using a decryption key that is totally unrelated to the encryption key.

According to cryptographers, this mode of encryption was developed during the 20th century. It was developed in order to overcome the challenges related to symmetric key cryptosystems. The main characteristics of this encryption scheme are:

- Each member of the cryptosystem should have two different keys – a public key and a private key. When one of these keys is used for encryption, the other one must be used for decryption.

- The private key is considered as confidential information. Each member must protect the private key at all times. The public key, on the other hand, can be shared with anyone. Thus, public keys can be placed in a public repository. As such, some people refer to this scheme as "public key encryption."

- Although the private and public keys are mathematically related, it is practically impossible to determine a key using its "partner."

- When Member1 wants to send information to Member2, he needs to do three things:

    o Obtain Member2's public key from the public repository.

    o Encrypt the message.

    o Transmit the message to Member2. Member2 will acquire the original message using his private key.

- This mode of encryption involves larger and longer keys. That means its encryption and decryption processes are slower compared to those of symmetric encryption.

- The asymmetric key encryption requires high processing power from the computers used in the cryptosystem.

Symmetric key encryption is easy to comprehend. The asymmetric one, however, is quite difficult to understand.

You may be wondering as to how the encryption and decryption keys become related and yet prevent intruders from acquiring a key using its "partner." The answer to this question lies in mathematical principles. Today, cryptographers can create encryption keys based on these principles. Actually, the concept of asymmetric key cryptography is new: system intruders are not yet familiar with how this encryption works.

Here is the main problem associated with asymmetric key cryptosystems:

- Each member needs to trust the cryptosystem. He/she has to believe that the public key used for the transmission is the correct one. That person must convince himself that the keys in the public repository are safe from system intruders.

  To secure the cryptosystem, companies often use a PKI (Public Key Infrastructure) that involves a reputable third party organization. This "outside organization" manages and proves the authenticity of the keys used in the system. The third party company has to protect the public keys and provide the correct ones to authorized cryptosystem members.

Because of the pros and cons of both encryption methods, business organizations combine them to create safer and practical security systems. Most of these businesses are in the communications and information technology industries.

Kerckhoff's Principle

During the 19th century, a Dutch cryptographer named Auguste Kerckhoff identified the requirements of a reliable cryptosystem. He stated that a cryptosystem must be secure even if everything related to it – except the keys – are available to the public. In addition, Mr. Kerckhoff established six principles in designing new cryptosystems. These principles are:

1. The cryptosystem needs to be unbreakable (i.e. in a practical sense). This excludes the system's vulnerability to mathematical intrusions.

2. The system should be secure enough that members can still use it even during an attack from unauthorized entities. The cryptosystem needs to allow authorized members to do what they need to do.

3. The keys used in the system must be easy to change, memorize, and communicate.

4. The resulting ciphertexts must be transmissible by unsecure channels such as telegraph.

5. The documents and devices used in the encryption system must be portable and easy to operate.

6. Lastly, the system must be user-friendly. It should not require high IQ or advanced memorization skills.

Modern cryptographers refer to the second rule as the Kerckhoff principle. They apply it in almost all encryption algorithms (e.g. AES, DES, etc.). Experts in this field consider these algorithms to be completely secure. In addition, these experts believe that the security of the transmitted message relies exclusively on the protection given to the private encryption keys used.

Maintaining the confidentiality of the encryption and decryption algorithms may prove to be a difficult problem. Actually, you can only keep these algorithms secret if you will share them with a few individuals.

Today, cryptography must meet the needs of internet users. Since more and more people gain access to hacking information and advanced computers, keeping an algorithm secret is extremely difficult. That means you should always use the principles given by Kerckhoff in designing your own cryptosystems.

Chapter 4: Different Types of Attacks on Cryptosystems

Nowadays, almost every aspect of human life is affected by information. Thus, it is necessary to safeguard important data from the intrusions of unauthorized parties. These intrusions (also called attacks) are usually classified based on the things done by the intruder. Currently, attacks are classified into two types: passive attacks and active attacks.

Passive Attacks

Passive attacks are designed to establish unauthorized access to certain pieces of information. For instance, activities such as data interception and tapping on a communication channel are considered as passive attacks.

These activities are inherently passive: they do not attempt to modify the message or destroy the channel of communication. They simply want to "steal" (i.e. see) the information being transmitted. Compared to stealing physical items, stealing data allows the legitimate owner (i.e. the receiver) to possess the information after the attack. It is important to note that passive data attacks are more harmful than stealing of physical items, since data theft may be unnoticed by the receiver.

Active Attacks

Active attacks are meant to alter or eliminate the information being sent. Here are some examples:

- Unauthorized modification of the message.

- Triggering unauthorized transmission of data.

- Modification of the data used for authentication purposes (e.g. timestamp, sender's information, etc.).

- Unauthorized removal of information.

- Preventing authorized people from accessing the information. This is known as "denial of service."

Modern cryptography arms people with the tools and methods for preventing the attacks explained above.

The Assumptions of a Cryptosystem Attacker

This section of the book will discuss two important things about system attacks: (1) cryptosystem environments and (2) the attacks used by unauthorized parties to infiltrate cryptosystems.

The Cryptosystem Environment

Before discussing the types of data attacks, it is important to understand the environment of cryptosystems. The intruder's knowledge and assumptions about this factor greatly influence his choices of possible attacks.

In the field of cryptography, three assumptions are made about the attacker and the cryptosystem itself. These assumptions are:

1. Information about the Encryption Method – Cryptosystem developers base their projects on two kinds of algorithms:

    i.   Public Algorithms – These algorithms share information with the public.

    ii.   Proprietary Algorithms – These algorithms keep the details of the cryptosystem within the organization. Only the users and designers can access information about the algorithm.

    When using a proprietary (or private) algorithm, cryptographers obtain security through obscurity. In general, these are developed by people within the organization and are not thoroughly checked for weaknesses. Thus, private algorithms may have loopholes that intruders can exploit.

    In addition, private algorithms limit the number of people that can join the system. You can't use them for modern communication. You should also remember Kerckoff's principle: "The encryption and decryption keys hold the security of the entire cryptosystem. The algorithms involved can be shared with the public."

    Thus, the first assumption is: "The attacker knows the encryption and decryption algorithms."

2. Obtainability of the Ciphertext – The ciphertext (i.e. the encrypted information) is transmitted through unsecured public channels. Because of this the second assumption is: "The attacker can access ciphertexts created by the cryptosystem."

3. Obtainability of the Ciphertext and the Plaintext – This assumption is more obscure than the previous one. In some situations, the attacker may obtain both the plaintext and the ciphertext. Here are some sample scenarios:

i.   The attacker convinces the sender to encrypt certain pieces of information and gets the resulting ciphertext.

ii. The recipient may share the decrypted information with the attacker. The attacker obtains the corresponding ciphertext from the communication channel used.

iii. The attacker may create pairs of plaintexts and ciphertexts using the encryption key. Since the encryption key is in the public domain, potential attackers can access it easily. It's a "hit and miss" type of tactic.

Cryptographic Attacks

Obviously, every attacker wants to break into the cryptosystem and obtain the plaintext. To fulfill this objective, the attacker simply needs to identify the decryption key. Obtaining the algorithms is easy since the information is available publicly.

This means the attacker focuses on obtaining the secret decryption key. Once he/she gets this information, the cryptosystem is broken (or compromised).

Cryptographic attacks are divided into several categories. These are:

- BFA (Brute Force Attack) – Here, the intruder tries to find the decryption key by entering all possible information. For instance, the key contains 8 bits. That means the total number of possible keys is 256 (i.e. 2^8). The attacker tries all of these keys in order to obtain the plaintext. The longer the key, the longer the time needed for successful decryption.

- COA (Ciphertext Only Attack) – This tactic requires the complete set of ciphertexts used for a message. When COA gets the plaintext from the given ciphertexts, the tactic is considered successful. Attackers may also get the corresponding encryption key using this attack.

- CPA (Chosen Plaintext Attack) – This attack requires the attacker to work on the plaintext he/she selected for encryption. Simply put, the attacker has the plaintext-ciphertext combination. It means the task of decrypting the information is easy and simple. It is the first part of the attack – convincing the sender to encrypt certain pieces of information – that presents the most difficulties.

- KPA (Known Plaintext Attack) – With this tactic, the attacker should know some parts of the plaintext. He/she has to use this knowledge to obtain the rest of the message.

- Birthday Attack – This is a subtype of the brute force approach. Attackers use this tactic when working against cryptographic hash functions. Once the intruder finds two inputs that produce similar values, a collision is said to occur: the hash function is broken and the system is breached.

- MIM Attack (Man in the Middle Attack) – This attack is particularly designed for public key cryptosystems. In general, these systems require the exchange of keys before the actual transmission of the ciphertext. Here is an example:

  o Member1 wants to send a message to Member2. To do this, he sends a request for Member2's public key.

  o An intruder blocks the request and sends his own public key.

  o Thus, the unauthorized party acquires the information that will be sent by Member1.

  o To avoid detection, the intruder encrypts the data again and sends it to Member2.

  o The intruder uses his own public key. That means Member2 will see the attacker's key instead of Member1's.

- SCA (Side Channel Attack) – This attack is used to exploit the weaknesses of a cryptosystem's physical implementation. Here, the attackers ignore the system's algorithms and digital protection.

- Fault Analysis Attacks – When using this attack, the intruder looks for errors produced by the system. He/she uses the resulting information to breach the system's defenses.

- Timing Attacks – Here, attackers use the fact that different calculations require different processing times. These people can acquire some data about the message processed by a computer system. They do this by measuring the time used by the computer in performing its calculations.

- Power Analysis Attacks – These attacks are similar to the previous one. However, instead of time, they use the amount of power consumed by the computer system. This information is used to determine the nature of the plaintext.

An Important Note About Cryptographic Attacks

The attacks explained above are theoretical and highly academic. Actually, most of those attacks are defined by cryptography instructors. Some of the attacks you read about involve unrealistic assumptions about the attacker and/or the system's environment.

However, these attacks have excellent potential. Attackers may find ways to improve them. It would be great if you will still consider these attacks when designing your own cryptosystems.

Chapter 5: Traditional Cryptography

You have learned about the basics of modern cryptography. You also discovered the different tools that you can use in designing your own cryptosystems. One of the powerful tools at your disposal is the symmetric key encryption: a mode of encryption that uses a single key for the entire communication process.

This chapter will discuss this mode further so you will know how to apply it in developing cryptosystems.

Old Cryptographic Systems

At this point, you have to study the cryptosystems used in the ancient times. These "old systems" share similar characteristics, which are:

- These cryptosystems are based on the symmetric mode of encryption.

- The message is protected using a single tool: confidentiality.

- These systems use alphabets to facilitate encryption. In contrast, modern cryptosystems use digital data and binary numbers to encrypt a message.

These old systems are called "ciphers." Basically, a cipher is just a group of procedures performed in order to encrypt and decrypt data. You may think of these procedures as the "algorithms" of these ancient cryptosystems.

1. The Caesar Cipher

This cipher is based on a single alphabet. Here, you can create a ciphertext just by replacing every letter of the message with a different one. Cryptologists consider this cipher as the simplest scheme today.

The Caesar Cipher is also called "shift cipher," since each letter is shifted by a fixed number. If you are using the English alphabet, you can use the numbers from 0 to 25. The people involved must choose a certain "shift number" before encoding the plaintext. The number will serve as the encryption and decryption key for the entire communication process.

How to Use the Shift Cipher

1. The sender and the receiver select a shift number.

2. The sender writes down the alphabet twice (i.e. a-z followed by a-z).

3. That person gets the plaintext and finds the appropriate letters. However, he moves the letters based on the shift number selected. For example, if

they are using the number 1, he will replace the letter "A"s with "B"s, the "B"s with "C"s, and so on.

4. The encryption procedure is done once all of the letters have been shifted.

5. The sender transmits the ciphertext to the receiver.

6. The receiver moves the letters of the ciphertext backwards, depending on the shift number being used.

7. Once all of the letters have been shifted, the decryption process is completed. The receiver can use the information he received from the sender.

The Cipher's Security Value

This is not a secure system since the possible encryption keys are extremely limited. If you are using the English alphabet, your possible keys are restricted to 25. This number is not enough for those who need more security. In this situation, an attacker may acquire your key just by carrying out a thorough key search.

2. The Simple Substitution Cipher

This is an improved version of the Caesar Cipher. Instead of using numbers to determine the ciphertext, you will choose your own equivalent for each letter of the alphabet. For instance, "A.C... X.Z" and "Z.X... C.A" are two simple permutations of the letters in the English alphabet.

Since this alphabet has 26 letters, the total permutations can be derived through this formula: 4×10^{26}. The people involved can select any of these permutations to create the ciphertext. The permutation scheme serves as the key for this cryptosystem.

How to Use this Cipher

1. Write down the letters from A to Z.

2. The involved parties choose a permutation for each letter. For example, they might replace the "A"s with "F"s, the "B" with "W", etc. These new letters don't need to have any logical or mathematical relationship with the letter they represent.

3. The sender encrypts the plaintext using the selected permutations.

4. The message is sent to the receiver.

5. The receiver decodes the ciphertext using the chosen permutations.

The Cipher's Security Value

This cipher is way much stronger than the Caesar Cipher. Even strong computer systems cannot decode the ciphertext since the possible permutations (i.e. 4×10^{26}) are too many. Cryptosystems based on this cipher can stop attackers that rely on a brute force approach. However, this substitution system is based on a simple scheme. In fact, attackers have succeeded in breaking letter permutations in the past.

The Monoalphabetic and Polyalphabetic Ciphers

Monoalphabetic Ciphers are ciphers that rely on a single encryption system. In other words, a single encryption alphabet is used for each "normal" alphabet throughout the entire communication process. For instance, if "C" is encoded as "X", "C" must be written as "X" each time it appears in the plaintext.

The two encryption systems discussed above belong to this type.

Polyalphabetic Ciphers, on the other hand, involve multiple encryption alphabets. The encryption alphabets may be switched at different segments of the encryption procedure. Here are two examples of polyalphabetic ciphers:

The Playfair Cipher

This encryption scheme uses pairs of letters to create encryption alphabets. Here, the people involved must create a table where letters are written down. The table used is a 5x5 square (i.e. 25 in total): the squares inside the table hold the letters of the alphabet. Since there are 26 letters in the English alphabet, a letter must be omitted. Cryptographers often omit the letter "J" when using this cipher.

The sender and the receiver must choose a certain keyword, say "lessons." They must write this keyword in the key table, from left to right. In addition, they should not repeat letters. Once the word is written down, the sender/receiver must complete the table using the unused letters (i.e. alphabetically arranged). With the word "lessons" as the keyword and J omitted, the key table should look like this:

L	E	S	O	N
A	B	C	D	F
G	H	I	K	M
P	Q	R	T	U
V	W	X	Y	Z

How to Use this Cipher

1. You should split the message into diagraphs (i.e. pairs of letters). If the total number of letters is an odd number, you should add a Z to the last letter. As an example, let's encrypt the word "human" using the key table created above. It will look like this:

HU MA NZ

2. Here are the encryption rules:

   a. If both letters are in the same column, you should use the letter under each one. You have to go back to the top if you are using the bottom letter. In our example, N and Z are in the same column. Thus, this pair becomes FN.

   b. If both letters are placed in the same row, use the letter located at the right of each one. You need to go back to the first letter of the row if you are working on the rightmost letter. (This rule doesn't apply to our example.)

   c. If none of the previous rules apply, create a rectangle using the pair of letters. Afterward, use the letters on the opposite corner of the correct letters. Work on the letters horizontally. According to this rule, the HU pair is converted to MQ (look at the key table). MA, on the other hand, becomes GF.

3. Using these rules, the word "human" becomes MQ GF FN when encrypted using the Playfair Cipher.

4. You just have to reverse the process if you want to decrypt the message.

The Playfair Cipher's Security Value

This scheme is stronger than the systems discussed earlier. Attackers will have a difficult time analyzing all of the possible keys. In general, cryptologists use this cipher to protect important information. Lots of people rely on the Playfair Cipher since it is easy to use and doesn't require special tools.

The Vigenere Cipher

This encryption scheme uses a word (also known as text string) as the key. This key is used to change the plaintext. For instance, let's use the word "human" as the key. You should convert each letter into its numeric value (i.e. A = 1, B = 2, etc.). In our example:

$$H = 8, U = 21, M = 13, A = 1, N = 14$$

How to Use this Cipher

1. If you want to encrypt "cold water," you have to write the letters down. Then, write the key numbers (i.e. 8, 21, 13, 1, and 14) under the words, one number for each letter. Repeat the numbers as necessary. It looks like this:

C	O	L	D	W	A	T	E	R
8	21	`13	1	14	8	21	13	1

2. Shift the letters of the normal alphabet according to the number written on the table. Here it is:

C	O	L	D	W	A	T	E	R
8	21	13	1	14	8	21	13	1
K	J	Y	E	K	I	O	R	S

3. As you can see, each letter of the plaintext is moved by a different amount – the amount is specified by the key. The letters of your key should be less than or equal to that of your message.

4. To decrypt the message, you just have to use the same key and shift the letters backward.

The Vigenere Cipher's Security Value

This cipher offers excellent security: better than the three ciphers discussed above. Cryptographers use this encryption system to protect military and political data. Because of its apparent invulnerability, security experts call this the "unbreakable cipher."

Chapter 6: Modern Cryptography Schemes

Nowadays, cryptographers use digital data to establish encryption systems. This data is often represented as sets of binary digits (also called "bits"). Modern cryptosystems must process these binary strings to create more strings. Symmetric encryption techniques are categorized based on the procedures performed on the digital information. These categories are:

Block Ciphers

These ciphers group the digital data into separate blocks and process them one at a time. The number of bits contained in a data block is predetermined and unchangeable. Two popular block ciphers, AES and DES, have block sizes of 128 and 64, respectively.

In general, a block cipher uses a set of plaintext data and produces a set of ciphertext data, usually of the same size. Once the block size is assigned, it can no longer be modified. The block size used for the system doesn't affect the strength of encryption techniques involved. The strength of this cipher relies on the length of its key.

Block Size

Although you can use any block size, there are some things you have to consider when working on this aspect of your cryptosystem. These are:

- Avoid small block sizes – Let's assume that a block size is equal to m. Here, the total number of possible plaintext combinations is 2^m. If an intruder acquires the plaintext data used for previous messages, he/she can initiate a "dictionary attack" against your cryptosystem. Dictionary attacks are performed by creating a dictionary of ciphertext and plaintext pairs generated using an encryption key. You should remember this simple rule: the smaller the block size, the weaker the system is against dictionary attacks.

- Don't use extremely large block sizes – Large block sizes mean more processing time for your computer system. Cryptographers working on large bit sizes experience efficiency issues. Often, the plaintext must be padded in order to get the desired block size.

- Use a block size that is a multiple of 8 – Computers can easily handle binary digits that are multiples of 8. You can take advantage of this fact by choosing a block size that has this mathematical property.

Different Types of Block Cipher Schemes

Cryptographers use a variety of block cipher encryption schemes in their systems. Here are some of the most popular block ciphers being used today:

- AES (Advanced Encryption Standard) – This cipher is based on Rijndael, an award-winning encryption algorithm.

- IDEA – This is considered as one of the strongest ciphers available. Its block size is equal to 64 while its key size is equal to 128 bits. Many applications utilize this encryption. For instance, the old versions of PGP (Pretty Good Privacy) protocol used IDEA extensively. Because of patent issues, the utilization of this encryption scheme is restricted.

- DES (Digital Encryption Standard) – This is the most popular block cipher during the 1990s. Because of their small size, DES ciphers are now considered as "broken ciphers."

Stream Ciphers

With this scheme, the information is encrypted one binary digit at a time. The resulting ciphertext is equivalent to the data processed (e.g. 10 bits of plaintext produce 10 bits of ciphertext). Basically, stream ciphers are block ciphers with a block size limit of 1 bit.

Chapter 7: The Pros and Cons of Cryptography

This chapter will discuss the pros and cons of using cryptography.

The Pros

Today, security experts consider cryptography as one of their most useful tools. It provides four things needed for modern communication:

1. Authentication – Cryptographic techniques like digital signatures prevent spoofing and data forgeries.

2. Confidentiality – Encryption schemes protect information from unauthorized parties.

3. Non-repudiation – The digital signatures used in cryptography prove the identity of the sender. Thus, disputes regarding this factor are prevented.

4. Data Integrity – Cryptography involves hash functions that can maintain the integrity of the data being transmitted.

The Cons

Nothing is perfect. Here are the problems associated with cryptography:

- Legitimate users may encounter issues when accessing well-encrypted information. This can turn into a disaster if a certain piece of information has to be obtained quickly.

- Constant availability of information – a basic aspect of communications and information technology – is hard to secure when using cryptography.

- Cryptosystems prevent selective access control. Some organizations need to provide exclusive file access to certain officers. When using cryptosystems, these organizations will have problems in giving selective access to their chosen members. This is because cryptosystems apply the same security measures on every file.

Conclusion

Thank you again for purchasing this book!

I hope this book was able to help you master the basics of cryptography.

The next step is to build your personal cryptosystems so you can easily encrypt messages.

Finally, if you enjoyed this book, please take the time to share your thoughts and post a review on Amazon. It'd be greatly appreciated!

Thank you and good luck!

www.ingramcontent.com/pod-product-compliance
Lightning Source LLC
Chambersburg PA
CBHW061027050326
40689CB00012B/2720